I0789162

The Story of a Special Day
Volume 104

April
13

The 103rd day of the year (104th in leap years). There are 262 days remaining until the end of the year.

by Michael Dobson

Timespinner
Press

This book is also available in e-book form for Kindle, e-pub devices, and other formats from your favorite online booksellers.

For more information about the series, about us, or about your special day, please email us at editor@timespinnerpress.com.

Look for other volumes in *The Story of a Special Day*, coming often. See www.timespinnerpress.com for details and for the most recent information.

Table of Contents

Cover: The crippled service module on the Apollo 13 mission. An oxygen tank exploded April 13, 1970, causing the lunar mission to be aborted — the COVER STORY.

Quote of the Day

"I would rather be exposed to the inconveniences attending too much liberty than to those attending too small a degree of it."

Thomas Jefferson
3rd President of the United States
born April 13, 1743,

Today
in
History
April 13

Pocahontas, by Simon van de Passe

What Happened on April 13?

From the creation of great works of engineering and art, to devastating wars and natural disasters, thousands of years of history have left their mark on each and every day of the year. Here are some important events that occurred on April 13. (Illustrated items are shaded.)

1613 — **Pocahontas is kidnapped** by Samuel Argall, who holds her hostage to ensure recovery of captives and property held by the Powhatan tribe.

1742 — **Handel's** *Messiah* is performed publicly for the first time..

1861 — The first battle of the American Civil War ends with the **surrender of Fort Sumter**, South Carolina, to the Confederacy.

1873 — On Easter Sunday, white southerners attack newly-freed slaves in Colfax, Louisiana, in one of the worst instances of racial violence during Reconstruction; over 100 African-Americans are killed in what becomes known as the **Colfax massacre**. No one is convicted of the crimes.

1902 — **J. C. Penney opens his first store** in Kemmerer, Wyoming.

1943 — **The Jefferson Memorial** in Washington, DC, is dedicated.

1953 — The CIA launches its mind control program, known as Project **MKUltra.**

1960 — The **first satellite navigation system**, Transit 1-B, is launched by the US Navy.

1964 — **Sidney Poitier** becomes the first African-American male to win an Academy Award for Best Actor.

1975 — In one of the first recorded racial mass shootings, seven African-Americans are shot by a white gunman in Wheaton, Maryland; two die.[*]

1997 — **Tiger Woods** becomes the youngest golfer to win the Masters Tournament.

2017 — The United States drops the **largest non-nuclear weapon in history** on Nangarhar Province, Afghanistan.

Apollo 13 crewmembers (left to right): James A Lovell, Jr. (commander), John L. Swigert, Jr., and Fred W. Haise, Jr.

---

[*] The story of the Wheaton Murders is told in a book of the same name from Timespinner Press.

Cover Story
Apollo 13 Crisis Begins (1970)

Apollo 13 Mission Insignia

Although the United States officially "won" the space race with Apollo 11 on July 20, 1969, there would be five more missions to the Moon, during four of which astronauts walked on the lunar surface. The exception was Apollo 13, the seventh manned mission in the program.

On April 11, 1970, at 13:13 Central Standard time, James A. Lovell Jr., John L. Swigert Jr., and Fred W. Haise Jr. lifted off on their mission to the moon. About 56 hours after takeoff, on April 13, there was a loud bang. Number 2 oxygen tank had exploded.

Over the next two hours, the entire oxygen supply of the service module was lost. The command module was left with backup battery power only.

The lunar module on Apollo 13, which served as a lifeboat for the astronauts for four days, is jettisoned toward the end of the mission.

Landing on the Moon was no longer an option, and there were many obstacles to be overcome so that the Apollo 13 crew could return to Earth. First, they had to make a course correction so they could use the Moon's gravity as a slingshot, requiring Jim Lovell to fly the spacecraft using only the sun in the cockpit window as an alignment star.

While there was plenty of oxygen in the lunar module, carbon dioxide removal required the use of lithium hydroxide canisters. An engineering team created a kludged-together system using plastic bags, cardboard, and tape to adapt canisters made for the command module for use in the LM.

Power supplies, water, and food were limited. The crew became dehydrated; Lovell lost 14 pounds.

The team managed to overcome one problem after another, but the toughest technical challenge came at the end of the mission. There had never been a case where the command module had to be powered up after a long sleep, and the flight controllers had to test and write new procedures to accomplish it, doing three months' work in three days. Even worse, by the time the Apollo 13 team reentered the command module, condensation had covered the interior with fine droplets of water. Water was inside the circuit panels as well, and the chance of a short circuit was all too real. Fortunately, safeguards against short circuits installed in the aftermath of Apollo 1 worked as planned.

As they entered the atmosphere, the heat of reentry created rain inside the command module. But that was the final hazard. On April 17, 1970, Apollo 13 splashed down safely in the Pacific.

Mission Control celebrates the successful return of Apollo 13

Quote of the Day

"We are all born mad. Some remain so."

Samuel Beckett, playwright and novelist
born April 13, 1906

Births
and
Deaths

THERI
ACA
MAGNA

April 13

The Wild Bunch in 1900 (seated, left to right); Harry Longabaugh (Sundance Kid), Ben Kilpatrick (Tall Texan), and **Butch Cassidy**. Standing (left to right): Will Carver, Harry Logan (Kid Curry), (Photo: John Swartz). **Butch Cassidy** was born April 13, 1866.

Notable April 13 People

With the current world population at about seven billion people, on average about 19 million people also celebrate their birthdays on April 13 — and that isn't counting the millions and millions who came before! No matter when you were born, you share your birthday with many special people whose accomplishments (and occasionally embarrassments) have been noted as part of history.

In this section, you'll meet fascinating people who share your birthday. They're organized by what they're famous for, and then in reverse chronological order from most recent to earliest. Those who are shown in photographs or artwork have a box around them. We don't have photos of everyone, so please forgive us if your favorite person is missing.

Some of these people you've heard of, others may be new to you, but they all make up an important part of the reason that April 13 is a truly special day!

Presidential portrait of Thomas Jefferson by Rembrandt Peale

Who Was Born on April 13?

Person of the Day
Thomas Jefferson (1743†)

Founding father of the United States, principal author of the Declaration of Independence, and third President of the United States, Thomas Jefferson is one of the most respected intellectuals in American history, and a leading proponent of democracy, republicanism, and individual rights.

Jefferson was born in Virginia, the third of ten children. He inherited a 5,000 acre plantation that included his future home, Monticello, at the age of 14, though did not take control until the age of 21. He attended the College of William & Mary in Williamsburg, studying math and philosophy, and after graduation earned a law license.

Although Jefferson himself owned slaves, as an attorney he worked for slavery reform and reprsented several freedom-seeking slaves with varying success. He married his third cousin, Martha, and the couple had six children. (Later in life he had a child with one of his slaves, Sally Hemings.)

---

† Because the switch from the Julian ("Old Style") calendar to the Gregorian ("New Style") calendar took place in the British Empire in 1752, Jefferson's Gregorian birthday of April 13, 1743, is April 2, 1743, on the Julian calendar in effect at the time of his birth. For more on calendar types, see "What Day of the Week is April 13?"

He built his palatial home, Monticello, still considered a masterpiece of Palladian style architecture.

The passage by the British Parliament of what were known in the colonies as the "Intolerable Acts" radicalized Jefferson. He was a delegate to the Second Continental Congress at the beginnings of the American Revolutionary War, and was made a member of the Committee of Five, responsible for drafting what became the Declaration of Independence.

Writing the Declaration of Independence, Jean Leon Gerome Ferris (left to right) Benjamin Franklin, **Thomas Jefferson,** John Adams)

Officially a colonel in the revolutionary army, Jefferson spent most of the war pursuing reforms in Virginia, serving as governor twice. After the war, he was appointed as a Virginia delegate to Congress under the Articles of Confederation. Upon adoption of the Constitution, Jefferson was Secretary of Statee under President George Washington, but was fired for opposing Alexander Hamilton's attemmpt to form a national bank.

He lost the subsequent election to replace Washington, and became vice-president under John Adams, with whom he did not get along. (Originally, the top electoral college vote-getter was elected President and the second Vice President, even if the two were from different parties.)

In 1800, Jefferson ran against John Adams, with Aaron Burr as his running mate. Jefferson and Burr, however, received an equal number of electoral college votes, throwing the decision into the House of Representatives. It took 36 ballots for the House to elect Jefferson president.

His most famous act as President was the Louisiana Purchase, which doubled the size of the United States. In a controversial move, he paid Napoleon $15 million to acquire more than 800,000 square miles of formerly French holdings.

In his second term as President, Jefferson was able to pass a law prohibiting the importation of slaves into the US, and attempted to purchase Florida for another $2 million.

After his presidency, Jefferson sold his personal library of some 6,500 books to the US government, forming the basis of the Library of Congress. He also founded the University of Virginia.

Thomas Jefferson and John Adams died on the same day, July 4, 1826. Adams, with whom Jefferson had reconciled, said on his deathbed, "Thomas Jefferson survives," unaware his friend and rival had died a few hours before.

His tombstone at Monticello reads, "Here was buried Thomas Jefferson, author of the Declaration of American independence, of the Statute of Virginia for Religious Freedom, and father of the University of Virginia."

But perhaps a better epitath came from President John F. Kennedy, speaking before a dinner honoring American Nobel Prize winners in 1962. "I think that this is the most extraordinary collection of talent, of human knowledge, that has ever been gathered together at the White House, with the possible exception of when Thomas Jefferson dined alone."

Jefferson Memorial (Photo: R. D. Smith, CC BY-SA 2.0)

Business and Industry

F. W. Woolworth, American businessman who created the F. W. Woolworth chain of 5¢ and 10¢ stores that featured fixed pricing on inexpensive items. *(1852)*

Antonio Meucci, Italian inventor who created a voice communications device that some credit as the first telephone. *(1808)*

Alexander Mitchell, blind Irish engineer who invented the "screw-pile lighthouse," allowing lighthouses and other structures to be built on mudbanks and shifting sands. *(1780)*

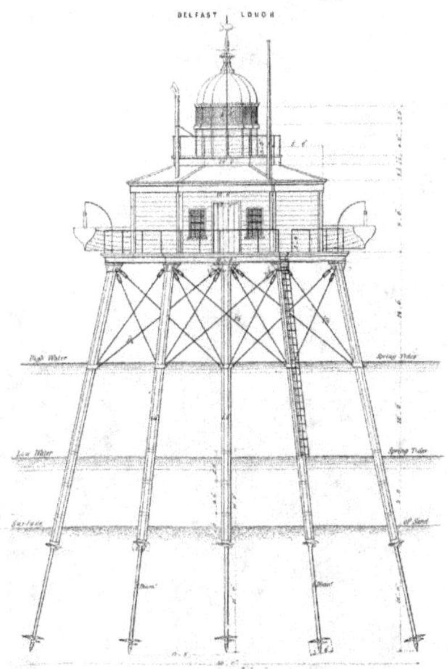

Drawing of the Belfast Lough screw-pile lighthouse, by Alexander Mitchell (1848)

Richard Trevithick, British engineer and inventor who developed the first high-pressure steam engine and built the first full-scale working railway steam locomotive. *(1771)*

Crime and Punishment

Butch Cassidy, American train and bank robber whose story was dramatized in several films, including 1969's *Butch Cassidy and the Sundance Kid* and *The Wild Bunch. (1866) (Photo page 10.)*

Guy Fawkes, famous for failing to blow up the British House of Lords in the Gunpowder Plot, an attempted Catholic rebellion. The date of the plot's failure and Fawkes's capture, November 5, has been celebrated as Guy Fawkes Day, in which his effigy is burned on a bonfire. *(1570)*

Guy Fawkes, by George Cruikshank

Government and Military

Orlando Letelier, Chilean economist, politician, and diplomat, assassinated with a car bomb by agents of the regime of Augusto Pinochet. *(1932)*

Harold Stassen, Minnesota governor best known as a perennial candidate for US president; ran nine times between 1944 and 1992. *(1907)*

Werner Voss, German World War I flying ace who achieved 48 victories, second only to Manfred von Richthoven. *(1897)*

Werner Voss

Sir Arthur "Bomber" Harris, commanded RAF Bomber Command during the strategic bombing campaign against Nazi Germany. *(1892)*

Journalism and Literature

Christopher Hitchens, author, social critic, and hournalist known for his confrontational debate style and strongly held opinions. *(1949)*

J. M. G. Le Clézio, French writer awarded the 2008 Nobel Prize in Literature. *(1939)*

Seamus Heaney, Irish poet and playwright awarded the 1995 Nobel Prize in Literature. *(1939)*

Eudora Welty, American writer who received the Pulitzer Prize and the Presidential Medal of Freedom for her many short stories and novels. *(1909)*

Marguerite Henry, children's book author best known for her 1942 novel *Misty of Chincoteague.* *(1902)*

Music

Lou Bega, musician best known for his 1999 remake of "Mambo No. 5.". *(1975)*

Marc Ford, lead guitarist of the rock band The Black Crowes. *(1966)*

Bill Conti, guitarist who was a founding member of the Red Hot Chili Peppers. *(1962)*

Jimmy Destri, songwriter and keyboardist for the rock band Blondie. *(1954)*

Max Weinberg, drummer best known for his work with Bruce Springsteen's E Street Band and as the bandleader for the shows *Late Night with Conan O'Brien* and *The Tonight Show with Conan O'Brien.* Member of the Rock and Roll Hall of Fame as part of the E Street Band. *(1951)*

Peabo Bryson, soul singer-songwriter whose hits include the 1992 theme from *Aladdin,* "A Whole New World," "If Ever You're In My Arms Again," and "Without You." *(1951)*

Al Green, singer-songwriter and producer best known for his soul hits including "Let's Stay Together," member of the Rock and Roll Hall of Fame. *(1946)*

Al Green

Jack Casady, bass guitarist for the rock bands Jefferson Airplane and Hot Tuna; inducted into the Rock and Roll Hall of Fame as a member of Jefferson Airplane. *(1944)*

Jefferson Airplane, 1967. **Jack Casady** is standing in the rear.

Bill Conti, composer and conductor best known for his film scores, including *Rocky, For Your Eyes Only, Dynasty,* and *The Right Stuff*; received an Oscar for Best Original Score for the latter. *(1942)*

Performing Arts

Glenn Howerton, actor best known as Dennis on the sitcom *It's Always Sunny in Philadelphia. (1976)*

Ricky Schroder, child star on the sitcom *Silver Spoons;* as an adult appeared in *Lonesome Dove* and *NYPD Blue. (1970)*

Ricky Schroder

Caroline Rhea, actress and talk show host best known as Hilda on the sitcom *Sabrina the Teenage Witch. (1964)*

Peter Davison, actor best known as the fifth Doctor on the long-running series *Doctor Who. (1951)*

Ron Perlman, actor best known for roles in the television series *Beauty and the Beast, Sons of Anarchy,* and the two *Hellboy* films. *(1950)*

Tony Dow, actor best known as Wally Cleaver on the sitcom *Leave It to Beaver. (1944)*

Tony Dow (right) with Jerry Mathers in *Leave It to Beaver*

Paul Sorvino, actor best known for roles in such films as *Goodfellows, Reds,* and *Nixon,* and for the television series *Law & Order. (1939)*

Lanford Wilson, playwright who received the 1980 Pulitzer Prize for Drama and was inducted into the Theater Hall of Fame and the American Academy of Arts and Letters. *(1937)*

Edward Fox, actor who played the Jackal in the 1973 film *The Day of the Jackal,* and the king in the 1978 television drama *Edward & Mrs. Simpson. (1937)*

Stanley Donen, director and choreographer called "the king of the Hollywood musical;" best known for such films as *Singin' in the Rain, On the Town, Royal Wedding,* and *Seven Brides for Seven Brothers. (1924)*

Don Adams, actor best known for his starring role in the 1960s sitcom *Get Smart;* also known as the voice of the animated character Inspector Gadget. *(1923)*

Don Adams with his shoe phone from *Get Smart*

Howard Keel, actor and singer known for numerous MGM musicals, including *Show Boat* and *Seven Brides for Seven Brothers*, starred in the TV series *Dallas*. *(1919)*

Samuel Beckett, Irish avant-garde novelist and playwright awarded the 1969 Nobel Prize in Literature. A key figure in the "theatre of the absurd," his best known play is *Waiting for Godot*. *(1906)*

Dadasaheb Torne, Indian director and producer who made the first feature film in India, known as the "father of Indian cinema." *(1890)*

Polymath‡

Philippe de Rothschild, member of the Rothschild banking dynasty, baron, Grand Prix racing driver, playwright and producer of stage and screen, poet, war hero, patron of the arts, and owner of one of the world's most successful wine labels, Château Mouton Rothschild. A number of his accomplishments were under different names to avoid trading on his fame. *(1902)*

Religion

Jack Chick, cartoonist and publisher best known for his sometimes controversial evangelistic and fundamentalist Christian booklets, of which over 750 million were sold. *(1924)*

---

‡ A "polymath" is someone who is expert in a wide range of subject areas, or known for accomplishments in many fields.

Roberto Calvi, known as "God's Banker" for his close association with the Holy See, chair of Banco Ambrosiano, which collapsed in a major political scandal, murdered in 1982 with numerous suspects but no convictions. Part of the motion picture *The Godfather Part III* is based on Calvi, especially the character Frederick Keinszig. *(1920)*

Madalyn Murray O'Hair, atheist and activist best known for her role in the Murray v. Curlett lawsuit that resulted in the Supreme Court ruling ending official Bible-reading in American public schools. *(1919)*

Saint Peter Faber, co-founder and first priest of the Society of Jesus (Jesuits). *(1506)*

Science and Technology

Michael Stuart Brown, American geneticist who shared the 1985 Nobel Prize in Physiology or Medicine for his work on the regulation of cholesterol metabolism. *(1941)*

Stanisław Marcin Ulam, Polish-American scientist who originated the Teller-Ulam design for thermonuclear weapons, developed the concept of cellular automaton and the Monte Carlo technique in statistics, and proved or developed numerous theorems in mathematics. *(1909)*

Sir Robert Watson-Watt, pioneer in radio direction finding and radar who developed the first practical radar device. *(1892)*

Sports and Games

Ted Washington, football nose tackle with the San Francisco 49ers, the Denver Broncos, and other teams; member of four Pro Bowl teams; nicknamed "Mount Washington" for his size. *(1968)*

Davis Love III, championship golfer elected to the World Golf Hall of Fame. *(1964)*

Garry Kasparov (Га́рри Каспа́ров), former World Chess Champion considered one of the all-time greats; remained the world's highest-rated chess player until his 2005 retirement; famously became the first human chess player to lose to a computer. *(1963)*

Dan Gurney, racing driver and team owner who as the first to win races in Sports Car, Formula One, NASCAR, and Indy Car categories. *(1931)*

Marilynn Smith, a founder of the LPGA and winner of numerous championships; member of the World Golf Hall of Fame. *(1929)*

Harold Osborn, American track and field athlete who was the first (and to date only) athlete to win Olympic gold medals in the decathalon and an individual event. *(1899)*

Alfred Mosher Butts, American architect best known for inventing the boardgame *Scrabble.* *(1899)*

Future chess grandmaster Garry Kasparov at age 11 (Photo: Owen Williams, The Kasparov Agency, © 2007 SMSI, CC BY-SA 3.0)

Boris Godunov

Who Died on April 13?

Government and Military

Boris Godunov (Бори́с Годуно́в), ruled the Tsardom of Russia as de facto regent before becoming Tsar himself in 1598. He is most often remembered as the subject of Alexander Pushkin's 1831 play *Boris Godunov,* later turned into a well-known opera of the same name. *(1605*[§]*)*

Journalism and Literature

Günter Grass, received the 1999 Nobel Prize in Literature; most famous work is *The Tin Drum*, made into an award-winning film. *(1941)*

Wallace Stegner, "the dean of Western writers," won a Pulitzer Prize in 1972 for *Angle of Repose* and the National Book Award in 1977 for *The Spectator Bird*. *(1993)*

Nicolas Chamfort, French writer primarily known for his epigrams and aphorisms. *(1794)*

Jean de La Fontaine, French poet primarily known for his *Fables*. *(1695)*

[§] Because of the switch from the Julian ("Old Style") calendar to the Gregorian ("New Style") calendar(see "What Day of the Week is April 13?"), the "Old Style" April 13, 1605 date of Godunov's death is equivalent to April 23, 1605 "New Style."

Music

Vincent Montana, Jr., drummer and composer called "the godfather of disco." *(2013)*

Johnnie Johnson, jazz, blues, and rock pianist inducted into the Rock and Roll Hall of Fame for his long collaboration with Chuck Berry; received a Congressional Gold Medal for breaking racial barriers in the US Marine Corps. Collaborated on numerous Chuck Berry hits and is thought to be the subject of "Johnny B. Goode." *(2005)*

Performing Arts

Larry Parks, played Al Jolson in *The Jolson Story* and its sequel; blacklisted during the McCarthy era for having been a member of a Communist cell. *(1794)*

Religion

John Humphrey Noyes, American minister, religious philosopher, and utopian socialist best known for founding the Oneida religious community in New York State. *(1886)*

Science

John Archibald Wheeler, American theoretical physicist noted for his work on general relativity; best known for creating the term "black hole" for certain stellar objects. *(2008)*

Annie Jump Cannon, American astronomer and suffragist instrumental in the creation of modern stellar classification systems. *(1941)*

Annie Jump Cannon

Sports

Dan Rooney, chairman of the Pittsburgh Steelers who served as US Ambassador to Ireland; member of the Pro Football Hall of Fame for contributions to the sport. *(2017)*

Nera White, basketball player named to the Naismith Memorial Basketball Hall of Fame and the Women's Basketball Hall of Fame, considered one of the greatest female players in history. *(2016)*

Thelma Coyne Long, winner of 19 grand slam titles and member of the International Tennis Hall of Fame. *(2015)*

Don Blasingame, second baseman for the St. Louis Cardinals, San Francisco Giants, and the Cincinnati Reds. *(2005)*

Quote of the Day

"The most completely wasted of all days is that in which we have not laughed."

Nicolas Chamfort, writer
died April 13, 1794

Holidays
Around
the World
THERI ACH MAGNA
April 13

La crucifixión by El Greco

April 13 Holidays and Celebrations

If you're looking for a reason to take your special day off, you should know that every single day is a holiday somewhere in the world! Here's some of what you can celebrate on April 13!

Easter Season

The Christian holiday of Easter in Western Christianity is held on the first Sunday after the Paschal Full Moon following the March equinox, which is officially set at March 21 by church reckoning. Easter itself can therefore occur as early as March 22 and as late as April 25, but occurs most often in April. In Eastern Christianity, which uses the Julian calendar, Easter occurs between April 4 and May 8. This also sets the date for the various events that lead up to Easter, especially the events of Holy Week.

Passion Sunday

The fifth Sunday of the Christian season of Lent is known as Passion Sunday in various Protestant denominations and by some traditionalist Catholics. Sometimes, the sixth Sunday of Lent is referred to as Passion Sunday, but it is more commonly known as Palm Sunday.

Passion Sunday starts the two-week Passiontide, which ends on Holy Saturday, the day before Easter, commemorating the day that Jesus's body was laid in the tomb. The fifth Sunday of Lent can occur as early as March 8 (though the next time it will be that early is in 2285 CE), and as late as April 11.

Palm Sunday

The moveable feast of Palm Sunday commemorates the triumphant entry of Jesus into Jerusalem, an event mentioned in all four gospels. In many Christian churches, palm leaves are distributed to the worshippers. The earliest date for Palm Sunday is March 15, and the latest is April 18.

Maundy Thursday

The Thursday before Easter is Maundy Thursday, when the Last Supper took place. The earliest day it can occur is March 19, and the latest is April 22.

Good Friday

Good Friday, observed during Holy Week on the Friday preceding Easter Sunday, commemorates the crucifixion of Jesus and his death at Calvary. The earliest day it can occur is March 20, and the latest is April 23.

Holy Saturday

Sometimes called Easter Eve or Black Saturday, Holy Saturday commemorates the day in which Jesus's body lay in the tomb. Some mistakenly refer to this day as "Easter Saturday," but that properly describes the Saturday following Easter, the last day of Easter Week. The earliest it can occur is March 21, and the latest is April 24.

Easter Eggs

Easter

Easter celebrates the resurrection of Jesus Christ on the third day after his crucifixion.

In the liturgical calendar, Easter follows the season of Lent, and begins the period known as Eastertide, which ends on Pentecost Sunday. Easter is observed religiously in a morning service.

In the U.S., it's also common to decorate Easter eggs and make Easter baskets of eggs and candy, often with the Easter bunny as a symbol. The White House traditionally hosts an egg hunt, and many communities have Easter parades.

Easter customs around the world include bonfires (Cyprus, western Sweden), men spanking women with a ceremonial whip (Czech Republic and Slovakia), egg fighting (Bulgaria), cross-country skiing and reading murder mysteries (Norway), and children dressed as witches collecting candy door-to-door (other Nordic countries).

Easter Monday

In some Roman Catholic and Eastern Orthodox cultures, the Monday after Easter is celebrated as a holiday.

It is also known in some countries as **Egg Nyte**, featuring egg rolling competitions and dousing other people with water that had been blessed with holy water the previous day at mass.

Easter Monday is also celebrated as **Family Day** in South Africa. In Guyana, people fly kites that were made on Holy Saturday. In Portugal, it is known as the **Anjo (Ivy) Festival**, in which people picnic in the countryside.

Śmigus-Dyngus (Poland, Hungary, Czech Republic, Slovakia)

The Monday after Easter in Poland and in the Polish diaspora is known as *Śmigus-Dyngus,* or simply Dyngus Day in the US. Boys throw water over girls they like and spank them with pussy willows. Girls avoid getting wet by giving boys "ransoms" of painted eggs.

Easter Week (Western Christianity)/Bright Week (Eastern Christianity)

The period from Easter Sunday to the following Saturday is known as **Easter Week** in Western Christianity and **Bright Week** in Eastern Christianity. **Easter Tuesday** is a public holiday in the Australian state of Tasmania. Because of the difference in the calculation of the date of Easter, Easter Week and Bright Week happen on different weeks each year.

A Bright Week procession

Other Religious Feast Days and Holidays

Passover (פסח) (Judaism, Samaritanism, Saint Thomas Christians)

Passover commemorates the liberation of the Israelites from slavery in ancient Egypt around 3,300 years ago. Its story is told in the Biblical book of Exodus, which is part of both the Jewish and Samaritan Torahs and the Christian Old Testament. Exodus tells how God inflicted ten plagues upon the ancient Egyptians before the Pharaoh would release its slaves. The tenth plague killed every Egyptian first-born child. Israelites marked the doorposts of their homes with the blood of a spring lamb so that the spirit of the Lord would "pass over" the first-born in those homes.

Passover is celebrated by Jews in a festive ritual dinner known as a Seder and by Samaritans with an animal sacrifice on Mount Gerizim.

For most celebrants, Passover begins on the 15th day of Nisan and ends on the 21st of Nisan in Israel and on the 22nd of Nisan outside of Israel. The earliest dates for Passover are between March 21 and March 27 (or 28), and the latest dates fall between April 20 and April 26 (or 27).

The First Passover Feast, by Huybrecht Beuckelaer

Saint Days

Each day in the year is considered a feast day for one or more saints. They are somewhat different in western Christianity (Catholicism and many forms of Protestantism) and in eastern (Orthodox) Christianity. There are many others; this is a selection.

In *Western Christianity*, April 13 is the feast day of Hermenegild and Pope Martin I.

In *Eastern Orthodox Christianity*, it is also the commemoration of Saints Theodosia the Princess, Martyrius, Ursus, Martius, Guinoch of Buchan, Arsenios of Elassonna, and Anastasia. (These saints are honored on March 31 by "Old Calendrists.**")

General Events

Deň Nespravodlivo Stíhaných (Slovakia)

Slovakia commemorates the dissolution of monasteries and the imprisonment of friars in Communist Czechoslovakia on April 13, 1950.

Dzień Pamięci Ofiar Zbrodni Katyńskiej (Poland)

Katyn Memorial Day in Poland marks the discovery on April 13, 1943, of the mass graves of the victims of the Katyn Massacre.

** "Old Calendrists" use the older Julian calendar rather than the modern Gregorian calendar for liturgical purposes. April 13 on the Julian calendar is the same day as March 31 on the Gregorian calendar. For more about the different types of calendars, see "What Day of the Week is April 13?"

New Year's Day (various calendars)

In many South Asian and Southeast Asian countries, the new year begins somewhere between April 13 and April 15, marking the beginning of spring.

Opening Day (Major League Baseball)

Major League Baseball generally begins its annual season on the first Monday in April (although it has been moved to different days to keep the World Series from extending into November).

President Woodrow Wilson throws the Opening Day pitch, 1916

Teacher's Day (Ecuador)

Many nations set aside a day to honor their teachers. In Ecuador, it is held on April 13 in honor of educator Juan Montalvo.

Friday the Thirteenth

While April 13 doesn't come on Friday every year, sooner or later, every 13th day of the month eventually lands on the dreaded last day of the week.

Friday the 13th is considered an unlucky day in many (but not all) Western nations. Both the number 13 and Friday have a history of being thought unlucky, so when you put the two togethe.... The idea that Friday is unlucky seems to be a maritime superstition — sailors believed it was unlucky to start a voyage on a Friday.

As far as the number 13 goes, there are a number of theories.One theory is that it refers to the 13 people around the table at the Last Supper, one of whom (Judas) would shortly betray Jesus. Others point out that on Friday, October 13, 1307, the Knights Templar were arrested, and many of them were later tortured and killed. In Norse mythology, Loki becomes the 13th guest when he crashes a party in Valhalla; the fallout results in the death of Baldur.

Fear of the number thirteen is common enough that a psychological condition, *triskaidekaphobia,* is named for it! (Fear of Friday the 13th is *paraskevidekatriaphobia.*)

According to some researchers, between 17 and 21 million people in the US alone are bothered by Friday 13th. Fear of thirteen is so common that many tall buildings skip 13 when numbering floors — over 80 percent of high-rise buildings in the US alone! Many hotels, hospitals, and airports don't have rooms or gates numbered 13 either.

(Photo: W. J. Pilsak, CC BY-SA 3.0)

Perhaps some of the bad luck associated with Friday 13th is self-inflicted. Fewer people drive on Friday 13th, but there are more accidents.

In Spanish-speaking countries, as well as in Greece, they worry about Tuesday 13th (*martes trece*) instead —though either way, January 13 qualifies. In Italy, though, 13 is a lucky number — but watch out for Friday the 17th!

In most of Asia, the number four is considered unlucky — the Chinese words for "four" and "death" are similar. Buildings in Asia may have a 13th floor, but often don't have a 4th floor.

Miss Rose Cade, "Queen of the Lemons," was nominated to be southern California's "Swat the Jinx" girl in 1920

Food Holidays

In the United States, almost every day of the year is dedicated to a particular food — some days honor more than one!. (Other countries also have official food days, but not one for each day.) Sponsored by manufacturers, retailers, farmers, or simply fans, these days are often proclaimed by the President, Congress, state governors, or mayors.

In the US, April 13 is **National Peach Cobbler Day.** Peach cobblers are a particularly American creation, invented by early settlers. It consists of a deep-dish pie with a thick (usually biscuit) crust and peach filling. Its rough look makes it appear "cobbled" together, hence the name. National Peach Cobbler Day was created by the Georgia Peach Council, which features the "World's Largest Peach Cobbler" each year at the annual Georgia Peach Festival.

Peach Cobbler (Photo: Ralph Daily CC BY-SA 2.0)

Honorary Food Months: *In addition, the entire month of April is used to celebrate numerous foods. Here's a list of food-related observances in the month of April!*

- National Florida Tomato Month
- National BLT Sandwich Month
- National Pecan Month
- National Soft Pretzel Month
- National Soyfoods Month
- National Grilled Cheese Month
- National Garlic Month

Honorary Months

Presidents, Congresses, and nations around the world issue proclamations recognizing particular months to honor certain causes. These events generally fall in April, though honorary months do come and go.

Two places to get up to date information are the current edition of Chase's Calendar of Events or the website Brownielocks. Here are some honorary designations for April.

- Alcohol Awareness Month (National Council on Alcoholism and Drug Dependence)
- Cancer Control Month
- Confederate History Month (Alabama, Florida, Georgia, Louisiana, Mississippi, Texas, Virginia)
- Earthquake Preparedness Month (California)
- Fair Housing Month
- Grange Month (National Grange)

- Holy Humor Month (Fellowship of Merry Christians)
- International Guitar Month
- Jazz Appreciation Month (Smithsonian Institution)
- Month of the Young Child® (Michigan Association for the Education of Young Children)
- National Arab-American Heritage Month
- National Autism Awareness Month (Autism Society of America)
- National Car Care Month (Car Care Council)
- National Child Abuse Prevention Month
- National Donate Life Month (Organ donations)
- National Frog Month
- National Greyhound Adoption Month
- National Kite Month (American Kiteflyers Association)
- National Landscape Architecture Month (American Society of Landscape Architects)
- National Poetry Month (Academy of American Poets)
- National Poetry Writing Month (NaPoWriMo)
- National Youth Sports Safety Month (National Youth Sports Safety Foundation)
- Parkinson's Disease Awareness Month (International)
- Prevention of Animal Cruelty Month (ASPCA)
- School Library Media Month (American Library Association)
- Sexual Assault Awareness and Prevention Month (National Sexual Violence Resource Center)

- Sports Eye Safety Month (American Academy of Ophthalmology)
- Straw Hat Month

Moveable and Multi-Day Events

Some events take place over a specific week or time period. Start and finish dates may vary from year to year. Some events occur on different days each year (such as "fourth Saturday of a month"). These events sometimes take place on or include April 13.

Second Week in April

- International Trombone Week
- National Dental Hygenists Week
- National Dog Bite Prevention Week
- National Library Week

Second Tuesday

- National Be Kind to Lawyers Week
- National Library Workers Day
- National Library Day

Third Wednesday

- National Bookmobile Day

Just for Fun

Anybody can make up a holiday, and many people do! While none of these are officially recognized and some may come and go, here are a few more holidays for April 13.

- Make Lunch Count Day
- Scrabble Day

Quote of the Day

"Oh, the lovely fickleness of an
April day!"

W. H. Gibson, *Pastoral Days*

About
the
Month
of

April

"April," from the *Brevarium Grimani* by Simon Bening (c.1510)

April: The Fourth Month

"I love the season well
When forest glades are teeming with bright forms,
Nor dark and many-folded clouds foretell
The coming on of storms."

> — *"An April Day," Henry Wadsworth Longfellow*

The origin of the name "April" (Latin: Aprilis) for the fourth month of the year is uncertain. Some say that it comes from the Latin verb aperire, meaning "to open," a reference to springtime. A similar word in Greek, ἀνοιξις (*anoixis*), meaning "opening" also refers to spring.

On the other hand, the Romans named many months after their gods, such as "January" for Janus and "March" (*Martius*) for Mars. The month of April was sacred to the goddess Venus (Aphrodite in Greek), and thus some think that April refers to her.

The fairy tale collector Jacob Grimm suggested that April came from the Etruscan name *Apru*, and believed that an Etruscan god or hero of that name gave rise to the month.

As the original Roman calendar started its new year in March, April was originally the second month of the year. It's uncertain when the Romans switched the new year to January, but it may have been as late as 153 BCE.

April is the springtime month in the northern hemisphere and fall in the southern hemisphere;

October is its opposite. It's one of only four calendar months with thirty days. Originally, April had only 29 days, but the calendar reforms of Julius Caesar (the Julian calendar[tt]) added the 30th day.

The first day of April and the first day of July always fall on the same day of the week; in leap years the first of January also falls on the same weekday as the first of April. In all years, the last day of April and the last day of December fall on the same weekday.

April in Other Cultures

The month of April has different names in different languages. Some nations use calendars other than the Gregorian, and their months may overlap with April. Still, they often have a word for April itself.

Albanian: Prill

Arabic (Egypt, Sudan, Yemen): مارأبريل (Abrīl)

Belarussian: красавік (Krasavik)

Bulgarian: април (April)

Chinese (Mandarin): 四月 (Sìyuè)

Croatian: Travanj

Czech: Duben

Finnish: Huhtikuu (burnwood month)

French: Avril

Greek: Αρίλιος (Aprílios)

[tt] . For more about the different types of calendars, see "What Day of the Week is April 13?

Hebrew: אפריל (Âprîl)

Hindi: अप्रैल (Aprail)

Irish (Gaelic): Aibreán mí Aibreáin

Italian: Aprile

Japanese: 四月 (Shigatsu)

Korean: 사월 (Saweol)

Lithuanian: Balandis

Old English: Ēastermōnaþ

Polish: Kwiecieńc

Russian: апрель (Aprel')

Scots: Apryle

Scottish Gaelic: an Giblean

Swahili: Aprili

Thai: เมษายน (Mesayon)

Ukrainian: квітень (Kviten')

Vietnamese: Tháng tư

April Sayings and Superstitions

Here are some sayings and superstitions associated with the month of April.

"April showers bring May flowers."

"If early April is foggy / Rain in June will make lanes boggy."

"When April blows its horn / 'Tis good for hay and corn."

"April wet — good wheat."

"Till April's dead, change not a thread."

"Marry in May and rue the day, but marry in April if you can, joy for maiden and for man." Which day? "Monday for wealth, Tuesday for health, Wednesday the best day of all, Thursday for losses, Friday for crosses, Saturday for no luck at all."

April Symbols

Birthstone: Diamond

Birth Flowers: Daisy and Sweet Pea

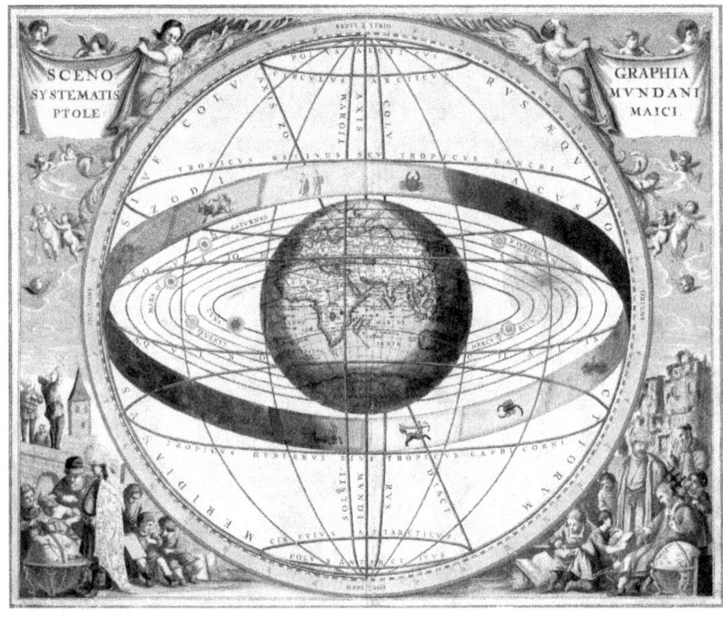

Scenography of the Ptolemaic Cosmography, by Johannes van Loon, based on Andreas Cellarius's *Harmonia Macrocosmica,* 1660

April 13 Zodiac Signs

From the perspective of someone on Earth, the Sun appears to move through the sky throughout the year, along a path astronomers call the *ecliptic plane.* The ecliptic plane is divided into twelve constellations, known as the zodiac, based on traditionally observed patterns of stars. On your birthday, you can't see your constellation, because it's in the daytime sky.

The zodiac was first developed by Babylonian astronomers about 2,500 years ago. Because they were unaware that the Earth wobbles like a spinning top (known as *precession*), they didn't make allowance for the fact that the Sun's path through the zodiac changes over time.

That means there are now two sets of dates for your birth sign. The *tropical dates* are the original Babylonian dates; the *sidereal dates* tell you where the Sun actually appears as it moves along its annual path.

For April 13, the tropical sign is **Aries** and the sidereal sign is **Pisces.**

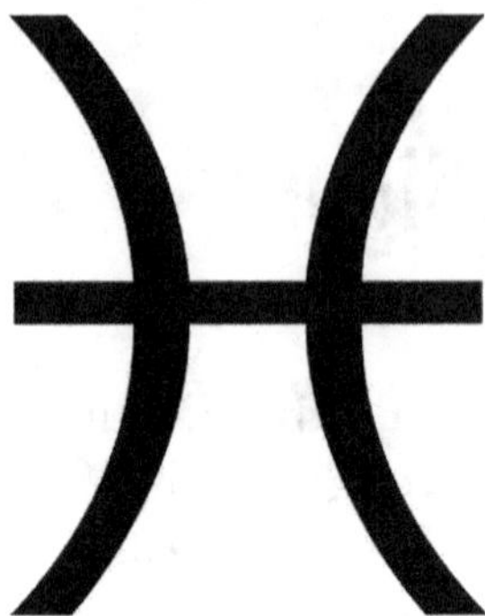

Pisces

Tropical February 20 to March 20
Sidereal March 15 to April 14

In the Roman legend of Venus and her son Cupid, they escaped the clutches of Typhon, known as the "father of all monsters," by transforming into fish and tying themselves together with rope. That's why the name Pisces is plural for fish. The constellation appears as a somewhat ragged "V" shape, representing the rope, with the "fish" located at the two rope ends.

In astrology, Pisces is a water sign, compatible with the other water signs Cancer and Scorpio, as well as with the earth signs Taurus, Virgo, and Capricorn. Pisceans are supposed to be imaginative, compassionate, unworldly, secretive, and escapist.

Aries

Tropical March 21 to April 19
Sidereal April 15 to May 15

In Greek mythology, Aries is a ram with golden wings and golden wool who rescued the twins Phrixus and Helle from certain death. Although Helle died in the rescue attempt, the grateful Phrixus sacrificed the ram to Zeus. The golden fleece from the sacrificed ram played a prominent part in the later myth of Jason and the Argonauts.

In astrology, Aries, a fire sign, is compatible with the other fire signs of Gemini, Leo, and Sagittarius, and to a lesser extent with air signs Scorpio and Libra. Arians are supposed to be adventurous, enthusiastic, quick-tempered, and impulsive.

Illustration by Edward Penfield

What Day of the Week is April 13?

On what day of the week does April 13 fall?

Surprisingly, this isn't an easy question. Because the calendar year is 365 days long (366 in leap years), it doesn't divide evenly by the seven days of the week.

Also, the Earth goes around the Sun in about 365-1/4 days, so a calendar tends to drift over time. That's why the same date falls on different weekdays in different years.

This is made even more complicated by a change in calendars that took place in 1582. Our modern calendar has its roots in ancient Rome, in a calendar reform conducted by Julius Caesar. Caesar commissioned mathematicians to attack the problem, and they came up with the idea of leap years, and thus standardized the calendar for centuries to come. This was called the Julian calendar.

Over time, however, the small errors in Caesar's calculation compounded. That's why Pope Gregory XIII commissioned the Gregorian calendar, used in most of the world today. Some countries converted in 1582, when the calendar was first developed; some converted later; other still haven't changed.

Gregorian and Julian aren't the only types of calendars. The Hebrew year, the Islamic year, and many other calendars are used in different parts of the world and among different people.

You can convert Gregorian dates to other calendars, including the Hebrew calendar, the Islamic calendar, and even the Mayan calendar by visiting the Fourmilab Calendar Converter at http://www.fourmilab.ch/documents/calendar/.

Chinese calendar systems are quite complex and have changed several times; a full discussion is far beyond the scope of this book. If you're interested, you can find information here: http://www.hermetic.ch/cal_stud/chinese_cal.htm.

On Names and Dates

Historians use "CE" (Common Era) and "BCE" (Before the Common Era) instead of the more common "AD" (Anno Domini, or Year of Our Lord) and "BC" (Before Christ), reflecting the fact that the year-numbering system established by the Gregorian calendar is used throughout the world in many countries not culturally Christian.

The CE/BCE designation dates back to at least 1708, and has been adopted as a standard by the United Nations and the Universal Postal Union. Because this series of books covers events and people of all nations and cultures, we use the CE/BCE terms.

The abbreviation "O.S." ("Old Style") and "N.S." ("New Style") on some dates refers to the fact that the Russian Empire (in particular) did not switch from the Julian to the Gregorian calendar at the same time as the rest of Europe, and therefore some figures and events have two dates.

Also, in the Julian calendar in England in the 16th century, the year began on March 25 rather than January 1. To avoid confusion with Gregorian dates, dates between January and March were often written using both years.

People and events whose original names are not in the Western alphabet have their native names (where possible) in the appropriate script shown in parenthesis. If you are using an e-reader to access an electronic version of this book, all characters don't always display on all devices.

A 50-year brass perpetual calendar.

Quote of the Day

"Time is an illusion, lunchtime doubly so."

Douglas Adams,
from *The Hitchhiker's Guide to the Galaxy*

Notes
and
Credits
Timespinner
Press

Cartoon by John T. McCutcheon

Copyright, Credit, and Contact

Follow Us

Our blog "This Day in History" (http://
timespinnerpress.com/this-day-in-history/) features short
articles on events and people associated with each day, and
updates several times each week. Also subscribe to the
"Quote of the Day" at http://timespinnerpress.com/quote-
of-the-day/. You can get daily links by following us on
Facebook at TimespinnerPress, or on Twitter as
@sidewisethinker.

Contact Us

Find an error or a format problem? Want information about
the series, about us, or about when the volume for your
special day might be available? Please email us at
editor@timespinnerpress.com. (We also take requests if your
special day isn't yet complete. Please give us at least six
weeks' notice if possible.)

Sources

We owe a great debt to Wikipedia, which is our first stop for
research. We attempt to make independent confirmation of
all important dates and facts through a variety of other
sources.

Other sources we frequently use include the Library of
Congress; "on this day" listings from *Encyclopedia Britannica*,
the *New York Times*, and the BBC; Omniglot for the names of
months in other languages; *Chase's Calendar of Events*; and, of
course, the always essential Google.

All art and photographs are either in the public domain, used under a Creative Commons license, or with a "fair use" justification, and most frequently come from Wikimedia Commons and the Library of Congress Prints and Photographs Division.

Attribution is provided where possible, or as requested by the copyright owner, or when there is particular historical significance, listed below. For information about any particular illustration or photograph, please contact us.

Credits

1. The cover photograph showing the crippled Apollo 13 service module is in the public domain as a work created solely by NASA. It carries the photo ID AS13-59-8500.

2. The illustration of the month of April used on the back cover is from the French Gothic illuminated manuscript *Les Très Riches Heures du duc de Berry* by the Limbourg Brothers, Jean Colombe, and an intermediate painter whose name is lost to history. It is in the public domain because its copyright has expired.

3. The box graphic used on the first page is from a 1916 pamphlet entitled "Divorce versus Democracy" authored by G. K. Chesterton, originally published in London by the Society of St. Peter and St. Paul. It is in the public domain in the US because it was published prior to 1923, and is in the public domain in all countries (including the country of origin) in which the copyright time is the author's life plus 70 years or less.

4. The graphic design for the section pages in this book is from a design originally created for a pharmacy label. It is courtesy of Wellcome Images (ICV No 11073, photo V0010813), and is used here under CC BY-SA 4.0.

5. The 1616 portrait of Pocahontas by Simon van de Passe is in the public domain because its copyright has expired. It is in the collection of the National Portrait Gallery, London.

6. The photograph of the Apollo 13 crew is in the public domain as a work created solely by NASA.

7. The Apollo 13 logo is in the public domain as a work created solely by NASA.

8. The photograph of Mission Control at the end of the Apollo 13 mission is in the public domain as a work solely created by NASA.

9. The 1900 photograph of the Wild Bunch by John Swartz is in the public domain because its copyright has expired.

10. The official 1800 Presidential portrait of Thomas Jefferson by Rembrandt Peale is in the public domain as a work created by an employee of the US government as part of that person's official duties.

11. The painting *Writing the Declaration of Independence* by Jean Leon Gerome Ferris is in the public domain because its copyright has expired. The image is in the Library of Congress, digital ID cph.3g09904. The original is in the possession of the Virginia Historical Society.

12. The 2004 photograph of the Jefferson Memorial is by R. D. Smith, and is used here under CC BY-SA 2.0.

13. The 1848 drawing of a screw-pile lighthouse was created by Alexander Mitchell. It is in the public domain because its copyright has expired.

14. The 1840 illustration of Guy Fawkes by George Cruikshank first appeared in a novel by William Harrison Ainsworth, *Guy Fawkes, or The Gunpowder Treason*. It is in the public domain because its copyright has expired.

15. The 1917 photograph of Werner Voss is in the public domain because its copyright has expired.

16. The 1973 publicity photograph of Al Green on *The Mike Douglas Show* is in the public domain because it was first published in the United States between 1923 and 1977 without a copyright notice. Traditionally, publicity photographs are not copyrighted because of the way in which they are intended to be used.

17. The 1967 image of the Jefferson Airplane was cropped from a trade ad for "White Rabbit" that first appeared in *Billboard* magazine. It is in the public domain because it was first published in the United States between 1923 and 1977 without a copyright notice.

18. The 1976 publicity photograph of Ricky Schroder is in the
    public domain because it was first published in the United
    States between 1923 and 1977 without a copyright notice.

19. The 1961 publicity photograph from *Leave It to Beaver* is in
    the public domain because it was first published in the
    United States between 1923 and 1977 without a copyright
    notice.

20. The 1968 publicity photograph of Don Adams in *Get Smart* is
    in the public domain because it was first published in the
    United States between 1923 and 1977 without a copyright
    notice.

21. The 1974 photograph of Garry Kasparov is copyright © 2007
    S. M. S. I., Inc. It was taken by Owen Williams, The
    Kasparov Agency, and is used here under CC BY-SA 3.0.

22. The 18th century portrait of Boris Godunov is in the public
    domain because its copyright has expired. The painter is
    unknown.

23. The 19th century photograph of Annie Jump Cannon is in the
    public domain because its copyright has expired. The image
    has been cropped.

24. The painting *La crucifixión* by El Greco is located in the
    Museo del Prado. It is in the public domain because its
    copyright has expired.

25. The photograph of Czechoslovakian Easter eggs was taken
    by Jan Kameníček, who has released the image into the
    public domain.

26. The 1988 photograph of a Bright Week procession is by
    George Rassasphore and is used here under the CC BY-SA
    1.0 license.

27. The 1563 painting *The First Passover Feast* by Huybrecht
    Beuckelaer is in the public domain because its copyright has
    expired.

28. The photograph of President Woodrow Wilson throwing the
    ball on the opening day of baseball season 1916 is a press
    photograph from the National Photo Company Collection,
    part of the Library of Congress Prints and Photographs
    Division, and is in the public domain because it was
    published prior to January 1, 1923.

29. The 1920 photograph of Miss Rose Cade is from the Keystone View Company. It is in the public domain because its copyright has expired.

30. The photograph of a calendar showing Friday the 13th was taken by W. J. Pilsak, and is used here under CC BY-SA 3.0)

31. The photograph of peach cobbler is by Ralph Daily, and used here uncer CC BY-SA 2.0.

32. The painting "April" is from the *Brevarium Grimani*, circa 1510, and is in the public domain because its copyright has expired.

33. The 1815 woodcut of a proposal is in the public domain because its copyright has expired.

34. The photograph of two diamonds grown by Washington Diamonds was taken by Inbai-Tania Studio, and is used here under the CC BY-SA 3.0 license.

35. The photograph of a daisy (*Bellis perennis*) was taken by André Karwath and is used here under the CC BY-SA 2.5 license.

36. The celestial sphere is from *Scenography of the Ptolemaic Cosmography*, by Johannes van Loon, based on Andreas Cellarius's *Harmonia Macrocosmica*, 1660. It is in the public domain because its copyright has expired.

37. The 1906 automobile calendar is by Edward Penfield, and is in the collection of the Library of Congress Prints and Photographs Division. It is in the public domain because its copyright has expired.

38. The 50-year perpetual calendar photograph is in the public domain.

39. The cartoon by John T. McCutcheon is from his 1905 collection *The Mysterious Stranger and Other Cartoons by John T. McCutcheon*. It is in the public domain because its copyright has expired.

40. The 1896 drawing "April" by Eugène Grasset is in the public domain because its copyright has expired.

License Description and Terms

Aside from material purely in the public domain, photographs and other material in this book are used under specific licenses permitting free use, usually with an attribution requirement. For full text and terms of these licenses, click or enter the appropriate links below. If you believe there is an error in the copyright status or attribution of any of these images, please email us.

- Creative Commons Attribution 2.0 Generic (CC-BY 2.0): http://creativecommons.org/licenses/by/2.0/deed.en
- Creative Commons Attribution-Share Alike 3.0 Generic (CC-BY-SA 3.0): http://creativecommons.org/licenses/by-sa/3.0/
- Creative Commons Attribution-Share Alike 2.5 Generic (CC-BY-SA 2.5): http://creativecommons.org/licenses/by-sa/2.5/deed.en
- Creative Commons Attribution-Share Alike 2.0 Generic (CC-BY-SA 2.0): http://creativecommons.org/licenses/by/2.0/deed.en
- Creative Commons Attribution-Share Alike 1.0 Generic (CC-BY-SA 1.0): http://creativecommons.org/licenses/by-sa/1.0/deed.en
- CC0 1.0 Universal (CC0 1.0) Public Domain Dedication (CC0 1.0) http://creativecommons.org/publicdomain/zero/1.0/deed.en
- GNU Free Documentation License (GFDL): http://en.wikipedia.org/wiki/Wikipedia:Text_of_the_GNU_Free_Documentation_License
- License Art Libre (Free Art License): http://artlibre.org

Other Books from Timespinner Press

The Story of a Special Day

Michael Dobson

A series of (eventually) 366 volumes covering everything that happened on your special day! Events, births, deaths, quotes, holidays, and much more. It's like a birthday card they'll never throw away!

US$7.95 print / US$2.99 ebook.

From Plassey to Pakistan

Humayun Mirza

The history of British Colonial India and the formation of Pakistan from the unique perspective of the son of Pakistan's first president and last of the royal line of Bengal, Bihar, and Orissa! This unique historical document tells the inside story of this distinguished family, including the detailed story of the coup that toppled his father from power!

US$27.95 print

A Whole New Navy: America's War in the Pacific

Miles Durr

The most comprehensive and detailed description of America's naval war in the Pacific ever—every battle, every ship, every task force and every task group from Pearl Harbor through the Japanese surrender! A must-have for the collection of every World War II buff!

US$29.95 print

Improbable History: The Weird, the Obscure, and the Strangely Important

edited by Michael Dobson

From the birth of Western civilization to the rescue of Apollo 13, from the Leaning Tower of Pisa to Florence's Duomo, history has often turned on small, improbable details. Whatever happened to the ancient Samaritan people? Why did a fortuitous rainstorm allow the British to conquer India? How did an air raid in Italy lead to the development of chemotherapy? What happened when Albert Einstein met Adolf Hitler on the streets of Berlin? How did the Japanese manage to attack the US mainland using balloons? A cast of award-winning writers tackle some of the strangest tales in history!

US$19.95 print

The Letters of William Philip Schwartz 1842-1855

edited by John F. Schwartz

The 19th century soldier and adventurer William Philip Schwartz wrote a series of vivid and detailed letters chronicling his adventures in the Indian Wars, the Mexican-American War, the Gold Rush, and his term as Marine sergeant aboard the USS Constellation. A pioneer in photography, he took *the first known war photographs*. An unforgettable first-hand look into life in the 19th century!

US$17.95 print

Timespinner
Press

www.timespinnerpress.com

"April" by Eugène Grasset